Resident Dog

INCREDIBLE HOMES AND THE DOGS THAT LIVE THERE

Resident Dog

NICOLE ENGLAND

CONTENTS

INTRODUCTION

Photographing people's homes on a regular basis, I soon realised that the shoots I enjoyed most were the ones where dogs were present. It didn't matter how imposing the architecture, how serious the home owner or how earnest the architect may be, some doggy hijinks could immediately bring an element of sociability, authenticity and fun to the day. Nothing lightens the mood like a nonchalant pup walking into frame just as you hit the shutter.

The photographs here represent some of the most incredible houses I've had the pleasure to shoot – with some of the most charming, adorable resident dogs. In these images, the dogs get to take us on a personal tour of their home. The presence of a dog allows us to see these homes in a completely different way. Whether they end up in the final shot or not, dogs can bring vitality, movement and warmth to sometimes static spaces.

Photographing dogs is not always straightforward. I know how to set up a shot so the architecture looks great, but getting a dog to sit (or stand or walk) when and where I want is another matter altogether. Most dogs are overjoyed to be involved, but that doesn't mean they are going to cooperate! The result is that these images end up with a looser, more spontaneous style.

I often wonder whether these pooches (many of them rescue dogs) comprehend just how lucky they are to live in these outstanding residences. Does Eric, a feisty little Yorkie, realise that his rooftop penthouse has won design awards around the world? Perhaps not, but these dogs do seem, on some level, to understand and appreciate the privileged lives they lead – at least, I like to think so.

One of my favourite shoots was at the peaceful residence of Ginger and Harry (page 160). Ginger, a reticent and elderly toy poodle, had recently found his quiet retirement interrupted by the arrival of a gregarious younger brother, Harry. Curious and unflagging, Harry followed the team around the whole day, energetically enticing us to play, at one point stealing the stylist's socks and dashing off with them in a bid to start a chase. Long-suffering Ginger, on the other hand, barely tolerated our presence. With their combined antics, our cheeks were sore from laughing by the end of the day.

Just as every home is different, so is every dog – but each one of them has that affability and enthusiasm for life that is the canine prerogative. The photographs here capture magnificent architecture and divine interiors, but within every frame, the dogs' idiosyncratic personalities can't help but shine through.

CHARLIE

Breed

Spoodle

Architect

SJB Melbourne

Location

Blairgowrie, Victoria

Modelled on a 1960s case study,
this light-filled home is spread over
five levels. The huge windows look
out onto a peaceful nature reserve.

For the most part, Charlie is a relaxed, easygoing kind of guy. It's only when he hits the beach that his renegade wolf side is revealed: chasing birds, digging holes and rolling in all manner of unsavoury things.

Reticent, shy and selective about his affections, Charlie is very much his own dog. He is a renowned bed hog and takes a brazen pleasure in hiding dog bones under the pillows of guests.

The interior of the house combines lots of natural tones with pops of colour, while warm cedar ceilings and walls contrast with cooler concrete and terrazzo surfaces. With his textured, cocoa-coloured coat, Charlie fits in perfectly.

SKIPPER

Breed

Border collie

Architect

Handelsmann + Khaw

Location

Hunters Hill, Sydney

Sensitive and responsive, Skipper has a knack for reading the mood of the household. He is a best friend to everyone: engaging, comforting and surprising.

Skipper's affectionate, loyal and gentlemanly presence brings happiness to everyone he meets. He is familiar with all the regular visitors to the house and knows everyone's routines.

Skipper can often be found sprawled across the large silk rug in the entry, keeping a sleepy eye on the family's comings and goings while enjoying the dappled sunlight. For a cattle dog, he's proven to be perfectly at home among the laid-back comforts of urban life.

The house is classic yet contemporary, with an industrial edge. It is designed to provide a calm retreat from busy city life. The family jokes that with his black and white coat, Skipper suits the monochromatic palette of the home.

On trips to the mountains or wine country, Skipper will happily tear around outside, especially if the weather is stormy. The beautifully curated garden at the North Shore property is not quite as forgiving of such behaviour and consequently his relationship with the gardeners is one of love–hate.

SCOUT, DIESEL AND BOSTON

––––––––––

Breed

Kelpies (Scout and Diesel)

Collie–Jack Russell (Boston)

Architect

MRTN

Location

Nulla Vale, Victoria

This country home is a retreat in every sense of the word. Sustainably built with mostly recycled and organic materials, it is totally off-grid and has a feeling of incredible calm and simplicity.

The three resident dogs are energetic, no-fuss, loyal and smart. Happy-go-lucky Diesel is always first to spot a kangaroo and set out in hot pursuit. Boston will sit at the window for hours staring down her arch nemesis, a placid white-faced cow. Scout, regal and well-behaved, likes to find a warm spot for a quiet nap.

Surrounded by rolling hills, the building's
high ceilings and big windows make the
cosy space feel spacious.

Perfectly at home in the rural
landscape, the house looks more
like a restoration than a new build.
It has the same quintessentially
Australian feel as the kelpie.

Concrete floors were chosen for their ability to withstand the scrambling of canine claws, while low windows mean the dogs can keep an eye on what's outside that might need chasing.

CANELA

Breed

Labrador

Architect

Andrés Casillas de Alba with Evolva

Location

Camberwell, Melbourne

A typical lab, Canela is loyal, warm, playful and happy. Offering unconditional companionship, she brings a reassuring, positive energy to this serene modernist home.

Canela loves people. She misses her family terribly when they go away on holidays (just seeing the suitcases come out can send her into a spin). When they return home, she's so excited she races around the living room in circles, sliding all over the soaped floorboards.

After a long walk or a dip in the pool,
Canela's favourite spot to nap is next
to the sofa in the main living area,
so she can be around her people –
but really any place will do.

Split over three levels, the house reflects
a warm minimalism with natural wood
tones offsetting the raw concrete walls.
Canela's only complaint is that there
are too many stairs.

COOKIE

———————

Breed
Labradoodle

Architect
Cavill

Location
Fortitude Valley, Brisbane

The house is a worker's cottage dating from the mid-1880s. It has recently been renovated, retaining the original façade but adding a contemporary extension at the rear.

Cookie has a robust personality.
She enjoys the company of humans
more than other dogs and loves
engaging with visitors. She'll choose
to sleep anywhere there's a person
sleeping – but guests are her priority.

Cookie has her very own futon to sit
on, which she likes placed so she can
view all entrances and exits to the house.
As long as she can keep an eye on the
goings-on of the household, she's content.

The grassed area at the back of the house, accessible from the living area, is one of Cookie's favourite places. Sometimes, though, she likes to sit up in the rooftop garden and take in the cityscape.

ENZO AND CARLO

———————

Breed

Italian greyhounds

Architect

Ian Moore

Location

Surry Hills, Sydney

Enzo and Carlo are refined, elegant dogs that are perfectly suited to the understated, sophisticated and timeless design of this converted warehouse.

While Enzo was rehomed, Carlo was adopted from a rescue shelter. When he was first let out of the car, of all the houses in the street, he seemed to know which home was his and ran to the front door.

The sleek, minimalist black-and-white
theme carries through all areas of the house.

Every element of the home was designed with the dogs in mind. They even have their own black leather beanbags for sleeping – though they're also partial to crisp white sheets.

THE RESIDENCE OF

BRUNO

Breed

Field spaniel

Architect

Kennedy Nolan

Location

North Melbourne, Melbourne

Bruno is a clever and amiable spaniel
in the prime of his life. He has a great
capacity for fun and loves car trips
and going new places. At home, this
loveable guy has managed to negotiate
four walks a day – he has an uncanny
ability to convey his wishes.

The Victorian terrace house has undergone several layers of renovations. The most recent work incorporates the owner's desire to create a quiet refuge from busy working life.

Timber, velvet, sisal, grasscloth, render and travertine create the rich, warm palette of the interior – Bruno's custom-built steel and perspex dog door is one of the few exceptions.

Cleverly designed, each room of this small, three-level home enjoys natural light, fresh air and a garden aspect.

The house wasn't really designed with dogs in mind, so it's lucky that Bruno is such a good boy: he doesn't jump on the furniture and, as a bonus, he's a handsome addition to the colour scheme.

CHARLOTTE AND FRANK

Breed

Toy poodles

Architect

Richards & Spence

Location

Clayfield, Brisbane

This light, modern home is, in all aspects, designed
for family living – and, of course, family includes pets.
A dog door was installed specifically for Charlotte,
although it was made big enough to accommodate
a terrier who sometimes came to stay (the builders
memorably nicknamed her 'Charlotte's fat friend').

At fourteen years of age, Charlotte is quiet,
sensible and loving. Frank, ten years her junior,
is not so quiet nor sensible but equally as loving.
Cheerful and gregarious by nature, Frank's
greatest love of all is food.

Charlotte and Frank like to be wherever
their humans are. When the family is away
from the house, the dogs lie on the step
inside the front entrance watching the door
and waiting to welcome them home.

MARS AND TRUFFLE

Breed

Lagotto Romagnolo

Architect

Multiplicity

Location

Hawthorn, Melbourne

Featuring bespoke finishes, contemporary art
and iconic furniture pieces, this home provides
an oasis of warmth for its young family.

The lagotto, also known as the Romagna water dog, has been bred in Italy for centuries – originally as retrievers and later as truffle hunters. With a loyal, friendly personality and hypoallergenic fur, the breed was the ideal choice for this urban family.

Mars and Truffle are half-siblings who adore each other and their human family. Mars has a calm nature and likes to laze around, while his sister, Truffle, has seemingly endless energy.

RITA

Breed
Standard poodle

Architect
Karen Abernethy

Location
Carlton, Melbourne

At just seven months old, Rita has brought
a breath of fresh air (and a lot of mess) to this
family home. She may be big on the outside,
but she's still only a puppy – she hates using
the suspended stairs and has been known to
get stuck halfway down, frozen with terror.

Always curious and cheeky, Rita is athletic, sociable, intelligent (when she chooses to be) and totally lovable. It is impossible for anyone to be in a temper when she's around.

The house is a place to which family members (and their dogs) return from near and far to be together. The original single-fronted terrace house has been renovated and a lofty extension and separate studio added at the rear. The light-filled spaces are designed for flexibility and can be used in myriad ways.

Rita's favourite place to sit is the living room, with her legs resting on the cool brick wall – from here she can observe all the activity of the household. She also likes to stand on the outdoor table and look into the house (or perhaps she's admiring her reflection in the glass).

Stewey is sweet, very loving and extremely
cheeky. His favourite game is to steal a cushion,
run outside with it and wait to be chased.
He is also an enthusiastic participant in family
cuddles, jumping on heads and nibbling on ears.

Having not quite outgrown his puppy phase yet, Stewey's moods swing from crazy to lazy. Generally he is one cruisy dude who would rather be at home with the family than venture out for a walk. He can usually be found lounging in a sunny spot or making himself comfortable on a couch or beanbag.

The architect designed a clever dog-door system so that there was no need to install one in any of the windows (of which there are many). When family members arrive home they can see Stewey waiting with toy in mouth to present to them as a welcome-home gift.

If Stewey could talk, he'd probably ask,
'What's with the weird stairs?'

Light and airy, the home allows the family (Stewey included) to be together without being in each other's pockets. The house is not large but its windows invite the light inside, making it feel spacious.

BERGIE

_____

Breed
Bull mastiff–kelpie

Architect
Hecker Guthrie

Location
East Melbourne, Melbourne

Due to his bull mastiff lineage, Bergie looks rather like a super-sized kelpie. Despite his striking appearance, he is extremely emotionally sensitive. In his old age he desires nothing more than the constant attention of his human – and treats.

The house is a compact late 19th-century Melbourne terrace. Modern modifications have delivered a pared back, neutral palette, which allows the owners to overhaul the interior design as often as they like.

Being a big dog in a relatively small space, Bergie's presence is always felt – for better or worse. He is vigilant in his role as protector, but when not on point duty he adds a relaxed and calming presence to the home. The kids absolutely adore him.

When the family is at home, Bergie's favourite spot is flat out in the centre of the living room rug, strategically placed not only to keep an eye on what's happening but also, most importantly, so he can't be forgotten.

Bergie was 'inherited' rather than chosen. Destined to be a working dog on a farm, he showed little inclination to uphold the legacy of his kelpie roots – plus, he soon outgrew his spot on the back of the quad bike. He seems more than happy to have ended up with this comfortable city life.

THE RESIDENCE OF

SASHA

———————

Breed
Rough collie

Architect
McBride Charles Ryan

Location
Prahran, Melbourne

With his regal manner and statuesque poise, Sasha's owners have nicknamed him 'Sir Galahad'. That said, the sound of a whipper snipper will send him racing around the garden in a decidedly undignified frenzy, barking madly.

This contemporary home is one of bold contrasts: dark polished-concrete floors, textured white ceilings, carpets in a range of vivid block colours and native-timber cabinetry. The custom-made mauve wool carpet upstairs is the perfect complement to Sasha's black, white and amber markings.

A courtyard separates the main house from an office at the rear. Sasha likes to wander between the two spaces and tends to sit with whoever needs some help de-stressing.

Sasha prefers to nap in the sun near the big glazed doors in the living area, so he can survey his backyard domain when he wakes.

The addition of Sasha to this household
was the result of a sustained campaign
by the family's youngest child – supported
wholeheartedly by the office staff.

THE RESIDENCE OF

M Y F

———————

Breed
Golden retriever

Architect
Vokes and Peters

Location
Bardon, Brisbane

From the day she arrived, Myf has been the happy centre of this home. She emits warmth, trust and love for everyone she meets.

The house has numerous vantage points from where Myf can view other rooms in order to monitor her humans (she has serious FOMO).

The house is a traditional Queensland 'timber and tin' cottage, thoughtfully adapted for modern living.

Myf's daily routine consists largely of finding and keeping the best spots in the house for sunbaking – and not moving for anyone (unless treats are involved).

Even for a dog, Myf has unbelievable hearing: from the very back of the garden she can hear the cheese drawer in the fridge open and will race upstairs to the kitchen quicker than you can say 'cheddar'.

GASTON

———————

Breed
Chihuahua cross

Architect
Room 11

Location
Fern Tree, Hobart

This small home, built on a steep
mountainside in southern Tasmania,
conceals a voluminous interior – and
one small, sandy-coloured chihuahua.

He may be tiny, but Gaston is bursting
with spritzy energy. He loves hunting
in the garden for the perfect stick
and proudly brings it inside for his
owners to admire.

The box-like building is referred to as the Little Big House. Stacked across two stepped levels to fit the sloping site, it has a compact footprint yet feels surprisingly spacious inside.

The only diminutive thing about Gaston
is his size. Even his name is larger than
life: Pluto Gaston Ferdinand Bailey.

HARRY AND DAISY

———————

Breed

Cairn terriers

Architect

Inarc

Location

Fitzroy, Melbourne

Harry and Daisy bring a softness, texture and gentleness to this modern Melbourne terrace house. They love watching the world go by from the front windows and soaking up the sun in the garden.

While they are half-siblings and look pretty similar, these two cairn terriers couldn't be more different. Harry is a boisterous boofhead, while Daisy is reserved and a little judgemental. Weirdly, when they lie down together, their bodies tend to form a perfect mirror image, right down to which leg is crossed over which.

Surrounded by lush landscaping, this home is full
of clean Scandinavian lines, with Japanese and
mid-century modern influences. The dominant
features are the monolithic staircase and a white
corrugated-steel feature wall; however, the dogs'
favourite feature appears to be the elevator.

APRIL AND MUFFY

Breed

Terriers

Architect

Zen

Location

South Yarra, Melbourne

April, a chihuahua–fox terrier cross, is a little pocket rocket: energetic, wilful and fiercely loyal. Muffy (aka The McMuffin or The Mufster) is a Jack Russell–silky terrier–cattle dog blend who resembles a friendly little Ewok.

Together, the dogs are frenetic, joyous, irrepressible and perhaps just slightly deranged. They love ricocheting through their dog door like bullets, chasing the cat or any other living creature that has the audacity to set foot in the backyard.

Like their house – a renovated single-fronted terrace house in the Botanic Gardens precinct of Melbourne – the dogs look small and unassuming on the outside but are full of personality. Unlike the dogs, the character of the house is wonderfully restrained, comfortable and relaxed.

GINGER AND HARRY

Breed

Toy poodles

Architect

Jackson Clements Burrows

Location

Elsternwick, Melbourne

Ginger and Harry bring fun, joy
and an unpredictable chaos to this
otherwise calm retreat. Lazing around
in the sun, they almost merge into
the architecture, while at other times
they literally bounce off the walls.

There are plenty of interesting nooks
and crannies for precocious, indefatigable
Harry to explore in this inner-city sanctuary.

Hidden within a secret garden, the house is made up of a series of layered and transparent spaces that allow the outdoor landscape to be enjoyed from every room. The honest palette uses durable natural materials like brick, concrete and white-stained timber (all robust enough to withstand young children as well as dogs).

Eleven-year-old Ginger (or Mr Handsome, as he's affectionately known) is the smart, composed statesman of the house. Harry, on the other hand, is a playful, cheeky toddler who always wants to be the centre of attention.

The dogs have full-run of the house.
A dog door concealed under the bench
in the meals area provides them
unfettered access to the large
private garden, where their favourite
activities include chasing birds,
tennis balls and frisbees.

CLAIRE

Breed

Kelpie

Architect

Coy Yiontis

Location

Balaclava, Melbourne

This is Claire's urban residence when her owner is travelling. The original Victorian weatherboard façade has been carefully restored and a modern and spacious two-storey timber-clad building added at the back. Travertine floors integrate the internal and external areas.

Having worked most of her life on a sheep
farm, Claire is well educated, intelligent and
unfailingly loyal. Now getting on in years
and officially retired, she still skips like a pup
in the mornings when it's time for a walk.

Claire has always been an outdoor dog, but in retirement she is allowed inside on special occasions or if there is a thunderstorm (which she hates). She'll even make herself comfortable on the sofa – but only if she's been given permission.

In her youth, Claire was an exemplary mother and bore several litters over the years. She never let her work slip, though – she persisted in going out with the farmer each day, racing home now and then to feed her hungry pups.

THE RESIDENCE OF

BUDDY

———————

Breed

Cocker spaniel cross greyhound–whippet–cattle dog

Architect

Bruce Rickard

Location

Clontarf, Sydney

Buddy is a young rescue dog with a
dual personality, balancing mad spurts
of energy with quiet, relaxed periods.
His offbeat personality and silly antics
keep the whole family entertained.

Designed in 1967, the house is built from recycled sandstock bricks and glass, with tallowwood floors and ceilings of western red cedar. There is an easy relationship between indoor and outdoor spaces, with generous shared living areas and smaller private rooms.

A real character, with his comical snaggle tooth and scruffy beard, Buddy finds the area's native wildlife to be a constant torment. He is fiercely protective of the family when strangers come to the door and has an irrational hatred of anyone in a high-vis vest.

DOUGAL

———————

Breed
German shorthaired pointer

Architect
Smart Design Studio

Location
Surry Hills, Sydney

Dougal likes to hang out downstairs
in the design studio. Luckily he doesn't
bark much or slobber, so he fits into
the office environment pretty well.

Eight years old, Dougal loves swimming, walking, playing ball and sitting on his humans. He is an affectionate fella and prefers to sleep in the middle of his owners' bed, snuggled under the covers, rather than in his custom-designed integrated kennel on the balcony.

The residence, directly above the studio, is a bright glass-pavilion shop top. Large windows look out to views of lush yellow robinia trees, giving the impression of being in a park rather than in the middle of Sydney's stylish Surry Hills.

THE RESIDENCE OF
POLLY AND PEDRO

———————

Breed
Jack Russells

Architect
Archier

Location
Yackandandah, Victoria

Pedro is a dedicated, gruff old dog with a unique aroma. He was inherited from a neighbour who passed away and still seems to prefer the company of elderly gentlemen over his adoptive family. Polly likes to lick faces – whether human, cat or Pedro.

Polly is like Pedro's shadow, but with better hearing and less farting. She loves warmth and sleeps away most of her day, often roasting herself under the wood heater. Pedro, on the other hand, would be comfortable in a hollow log and often chooses to sleep in the workshop.

ZARA

Breed

Staffordshire bull terrier

Architect

Ciaran Acton and David Whittaker/Hassell

Location

Rozelle, Sydney

Zara is a chilled-out dog who loves belly scratches, food, walks and sleeping – but most of all she likes to be wherever her humans are. She is great with kids, easy to train and her beautiful blue coat doesn't shed.

A welcome-home greeting from
Zara is a delight, with lots of excited
jumping, barking and licking.

The modest home is partially surrounded by
a brick retaining wall that was built in 1929
to support a community grandstand. Inside,
birch ply and burnt-ash timber linings combine
with concrete floors and glass openings
throughout to create a simple, warm palette.

MUDDY

———————

Breed

Labradoodle

Architect

Tonkin Zulaikha Greer

Location

Balmain East, Sydney

Muddy's residence is a pavilion that overlooks the harbour, the interior connecting seamlessly with the garden and surrounding landscape.

Gentle and devoted, Muddy is seemingly tuned in to the thoughts of his humans, appearing to understand their every desire and command. (Whether he chooses to obey or not is another matter altogether.)

Muddy was chosen by this family
because labradoodles are known
to be friendly, intelligent dogs.

With his shaggy cappuccino coat,
Muddy fits in nicely among the
imperfect, impermanent and
incomplete elements of the home.

At night, Muddy sleeps in his own
bed on the floor of the master suite.
During the day, Muddy will carry his
bed from room to room so he can nap
in adequate proximity to the family.

This clever dog has learnt to slide open
one of the downstairs windows so he
can let himself out to enjoy the wildness
of the garden and say hello to visitors.

From his vantage point looking out over the park and laneway, Muddy vigilantly surveils the area, protecting his owners from intruding dogs and possums.

ERIC

Breed

Yorkshire terrier

Architect

SJB Sydney

Location

Redfern, Sydney

Dogmatic, cheeky and opinionated,
Eric is generally uninterested
in other people's business.

The penthouse apartment is nestled among a garden in the sky. Calm and comfortable, it is a sanctuary in the middle of the city.

Located on the rooftop of a converted machinery manufacturing plant, the home is full of drama and surprises – like the statement emerald-green kitchen. The compact master bedroom, ensuite and study are secreted away in what was originally the goods lift.

Eric's owners thoughtfully ensured the rooftop
garden included some grass for him, but they
needn't have bothered – it turns out he hates
getting his feet wet. He prefers to enjoy the
outdoors from the comfort of a backpack.

A little dog in a big world, Eric likes to sleep in the custom 'mouse hole' carved into the base of his owners' bed, where he feels safe and protected.

ARTWORK CREDITS

ACKNOWLEDGEMENTS

———————

I would like to thank all the people who made this book possible. Thank you for the incredible enthusiasm from not only my friends and family, but also everybody involved. The book would not be possible without the support and shared vision of my publishers, the architects and clients for believing in the idea, and most importantly, all the beautiful resident dogs.

I would like to acknowledge: Christina Force who set me on this path, Natalie James and Swee Lim for their incredible eye for styling the majority of these homes, Stephen Ellinghaus for the name, Jessica Redman for her beautiful words, Jacinta Lippold for her understated elegant book design, Greg Ross for his technical eye for image perfection, Stephen Crafti for the introduction, Paulina de Laveaux for jumping on board so quickly and Kirsten Abbott for following it through. And of course, it goes without saying, thank you to my partner, Rick Kersley.

A special thank you to Marita Foley, Hamish Guthrie, Patrick Kennedy, Karen McCartney and David Harrison, Andrew and Victoria Greensmith, Andrew Parr and Stacey Pavlou, Jennifer and Michael Bergman, Rosa Coy and George Yiontis, Helen Cavill, William Smart, Tess Strelein and Ian Moore, Adam Haddow, Megan Baynes and Thomas Bailey, Graham and Dana Burrows, Liz and Stuart Crosby, Brian Zulaikha and Janet Laurence, Allison Manvell and Simon Jenkins, Ben Gilbert, Karen Abernethy, Michelle Bennett and Louise Lovering, the McKenzie Gregg family, Georgina and Nick Stamford, Tyrone and Taryn Gabriel, Terry Wu, and Debbie-Lyn Ryan.

Thank you again to Thames & Hudson for believing in this project and for bringing it to life.

THE AUTHOR

Nicole England is a Melbourne-based architecture and interiors photographer who has worked with many of the industry's top architects and designers, both in Australia and abroad. A graduate of the highly regarded Elam School of Fine Arts within the University of Auckland, she has an intimate understanding of light and form, and a sharp eye for composition. Her photography brings the everyday spaces we inhabit into focus, highlighting the artistry and the beauty that is often overlooked.

Her work has graced the glossy pages of magazines worldwide, including *Architectural Digest, Elle Decor, Wallpaper, Vogue Living, Artichoke, Inside* and *Indesign*.

THE ARCHITECTS

Andrés Casillas de Alba with Evolva – evolva.com.au

Archier – archier.com.au

Austin Maynard – maynardarchitects.com

Bruce Rickard (1929–2010)

Cavill – cavillarchitects.com

Ciaran Acton and David Whittaker/Hassell – hassellstudio.com

Coy Yiontis – coyyiontis.com.au

Handelsmann + Khaw – handelsmannkhaw.com

Hecker Guthrie – heckerguthrie.com

Ian Moore – ianmoorearchitects.com

Inarc – inarc.com.au

Jackson Clements Burrows – jcba.com.au

Karen Abernethy – karenabernethy.com

Kennedy Nolan – kennedynolan.com.au

McBride Charles Ryan – mcbridecharlesryan.com.au

MRTN – mrtn.com.au

Multiplicity – multiplicity.com.au

Richards & Spence – richardsandspence.com

Room 11 – room11.com.au

SJB Melbourne/Sydney – sjb.com.au

Smart Design Studio – smartdesignstudio.com

Tonkin Zulaikha Greer – tzg.com.au

Vokes and Peters – vokesandpeters.com

Zen – zenarchitects.com

First published in the United States of America in 2019

This compact edition published in the United States
of America in 2021 by Thames & Hudson Inc.,
500 Fifth Avenue, New York, New York 10110

Reprinted in 2021

www.thamesandhudsonusa.com

©Thames & Hudson Australia 2020
Text and images © Nicole England 2018

Library of Congress Control Number 2018965636

ISBN 978-1-760-76131-8

Every effort has been made to trace accurate ownership
of copyrighted text and visual materials used in this book.
Errors or omissions will be corrected in subsequent
editions, provided notification is sent to the publisher.

Design — JAC&
Editing — Jessica Redman
Printed and bound in China by RR Donnelley

FSC® is dedicated to the promotion of responsible forest
management worldwide. This book is made of material from
FSC®-certified forests and other controlled sources.